WRITING FITNESS

Practical Exercises for Better Business Writing

Jack Swenson

A FIFTY-MINUTE™ SERIES BOOK

CRISP PUBLICATIONS, INC.
Menlo Park, California

ABOUT THIS BOOK

WRITING FITNESS is not like most books. It has a unique "self-paced" format that encourages a reader to become personally involved. Designed to be "read with a pencil," there are an abundance of exercises and activities that invite participation.

The objective of WRITING FITNESS is to help people improve the quality of their business-writing skills by providing basic concepts and allowing the readers to practice what they have learned.

WRITING FITNESS is valuable in several ways. Here are some possibilities:

—**Individual Study.** Because the book is self-instructional, all that is needed is a quiet place, some time, and a pencil. Completing the activities and exercises will provide practical steps for self-improvement.

—**Workshops and Seminars.** This book is ideal as pre-assigned reading prior to a formal training session. With the basics in hand, more time can be spent on concept extensions and advanced applications. The book is also effective when used as part of a workshop or seminar.

—**Remote Location Training.** Copies can be sent to those not able to attend "home office" training sessions. WRITING FITNESS also makes an excellent "desk reference book."

There are other possibilities depending on the specific needs or objectives of the user. WRITING FITNESS is an excellent companion volume to BETTER BUSINESS WRITING which may be ordered from the back of the book.

CONTENTS

PART I—INTRODUCTION

INTRODUCTION

Writing Skills Are Essential

Anyone who earns a living at a desk knows how important it is to have good writing skills. A good letter can get you a job interview or win you a new client. An ability to write clear, concise memos and reports can help you move up the ladder in your organization and win you a better job. On the other hand, poor writing wastes time and costs money. As one consultant recently said, ''Profits improve only when our correspondence is read. No sale is made when a business letter ends up in the wastebasket.''

A High-Tech World

There has always been a need for clear communication in business. A poorly worded letter will either cause confusion or leave a poor impression. A muddled memo can result in misunderstanding or lead to employee grievances. A sloppy report will often result in lost business.

Part of the challenge of clear writing is the nature of business communication. Business writing is often necessarily technical and complex. This kind of writing makes special demands on a writer. A writer who has not yet learned to have sympathy for the reader is bound to create problems for himself or herself.

Has something like this ever happened to you? It's a true story. An accountant sent a letter to a client explaining a service that had been performed for the customer. A few days later the client called. ''Thanks for the letter,'' the client said. ''Now tell me what you said.'' Embarrassing? Yes. And worse. No wonder business executives are concerned about the effect of poor writing skills on profitability.

But isn't writing ability less important in today's high-tech world of computers and electronic data processing? Don't we now depend more on machines for precise, accurate communication? The experts say no. They maintain that good communication skills are more critical than ever. The spread of electronic communication devices makes better writing imperative. Size, too, is having an impact on today's business needs. As *Business Week* pointed out (July 6, 1981), ''the ability to write simple direct prose that says precisely what you want it to say in the fewest words. . .has become rare—just when business and social organizations have grown too large for anyone to be effective face-to-face.''

Writing Fitness

This book can help you develop the business writing skills you need to succeed. It is a book of exercises for busy people who want to write better memos, letters, and reports. The exercises are designed to tone and strengthen a writer's style, just like physical exercise and diet are used to build a healthy body. This book explains how to slim down sentences to make the meaning clearer. It shows how to choose stronger words. *Writing Fitness* can help anyone learn to write a clear, concise memo, persuasive letter, or well-organized report.

Better Writing Now

Some readers may have reservations about the length of time it takes to develop good writing habits. You may believe it takes years to become a good writer. You may be reluctant to commit yourself to the time and effort you feel are necessary. Let's give that myth a decent burial right away. True, it takes time and energy to become an accomplished writer. No professional writer ever got to that level without using up a lot of pencils, paper, and ink. But it does *not* take years or even months to become a good writer. Most people can make remarkable progress in a few weeks. Indeed, you should *expect* to see significant improvement quickly. The principles of effective writing are simple and easy to apply. You can prove to yourself that it is possible to learn to be a better writer by performing this simple test. Dig a letter or memo out of your files; it doesn't matter if you wrote it or it was written by somebody else. Then, pen or pencil in hand, go over the document sentence by sentence, *crossing out any words unnecessary to make the meaning clear*. When you have finished, compare the two versions. Read them aloud. Which looks and sounds better? Odds are it will be the one that is shorter and more concise.

Some Helpful Resources

If you want to begin developing better writing skills, you don't have to sign up for a course or wade through a grammar book. All you have to do is apply a few simple principles of effective writing. This book will help you do that. For readers who have the time and desire to pursue the matter of writing improvement further, I strongly recommend the entire series of articles printed as advertisements by International Paper Company. Of particular interest to business writers are "How to Write with Style" by Kurt Vonnegut, "How to Write Clearly" by Edward Thompson, "How to Write a Business Letter" by Malcolm Forbes, and "How to Punctuate" by Russell Baker. Doubleday has now published 13 of the two page articles in a book titled *How to Use the Power of the Printed Word*. For information write to International Paper Co., Dept. 16Z, P.O. Box 954, Madison Sq. Sta., N.Y., NY 10010.

Some other books that will also help you build your skills as a writer are *Elements of Style* by Strunk and White, *On Writing Well* by William Zinsser, and *Better Business Writing* by Susan L. Brock. A grammar handbook is also handy. An excellent, brief manual that contains all you need to know about English grammar and usage is *English Simplified* by Blanche Ellsworth.

About the Organization of This Book

Writing Fitness will get your writing muscles in shape. It will help tone your prose style and get rid of the fatty deposits in your sentences. It will help you select words that make your writing more vital. This book contains a series of exercises and activities in a "self-study" format. Suggested answers and model responses follow the exercises for immediate reinforcement. Parts II and III will help you improve the wording of phrases and sentences. Parts IV, V, and VI contain sample memos, letters, and a business report for you to revise, and Part VII contains a series of assignments to help you produce improved business correspondence.

PART II—SOME BASICS OF STYLE

SOME BASICS OF STYLE

Building a Foundation

Many writers have trouble with basics such as spelling, punctuation, grammar, and mechanics. It's no disgrace to be a poor speller, just a handicap. A good beginning point for a self-improvement course on writing is with the basics of the language. If you are weak in this area, the first step is to admit it. Then begin to build a foundation for improved skill with the language. A grammar handbook is a useful reference. You can also benefit by making it a habit to look up words you don't know how to spell in the dictionary and writing them several times until you learn them.

One Step at a Time

If your basic skills are weak, don't despair. Learning how to write is like everything else: it must be learned one step at a time. Isolate your biggest weakness and deal with it first. This section of the book will help you start building the basic skills you need. The purpose of this section is to point you in the right direction. You will discover how to use the dictionary correctly. You will also learn some spelling shortcuts and review the four most important spelling rules. Punctuation and mechanics are also covered, including the correct use of apostrophes, when to use capital letters, use of italics, and placement of commas and periods in quotations. Finally, there is a quiz on usage. Have some fun and give this quiz to your friends: see how smart *they* are!

EXERCISE SECTION

The following exercises will provide you with an opportunity to answer questions related to various writing skills. Answers to the questions for individual exercises will be found on the page following the exercise.

At this stage, it is not important how many you answer correctly. The primary purpose for the exercises is to provide you with some instant feedback about problem areas where you may need additional help. In addition to the suggestions given in this book about how to improve your writing skills, don't forget other (more comprehensive) resources are available. A few of the best were noted on page 3.

EXERCISES AHEAD

EXERCISE # 1—SPELLING

Are you a poor speller? Here's an easy way to fix the proper spelling of a word in your mind. First, look up the problem word in the dictionary. Note that the word is broken down into syllables (psy•chol•o•gy). *Look* at the word; look at each syllable one at a time. Next *say* the word aloud, pronouncing each syllable (''sigh-kol-oh-gee''). Next, close your eyes and visualize the word in your mind's eye. Again, say the word aloud. Finally, *write* the word correctly on a sheet of paper. If necessary, write the word several times.

The sentences below contain ten words commonly misspelled in business communication. Correctly spell the word in brackets. (Note: hyphens *may or may not* indicate missing letters.) Compare your answers with the correctly spelled words on the next page. Look up any words you misspelled. Memorize the correct spelling using the procedure outlined above.

1. Your request is not (consist-nt) with company policy.

2. The meeting will be in our branch office near the (capit-l) building.

3. An (exten-ion) of benefits will be offered to all employees.

4. Compensation and benefits are (sep-rate) issues.

5. The new policy will (super-ede) the old one.

6. Please refer to the instructions on the (pre-ding) page.

7. The manager said that it (oc-ur-ed) to him that the employees needed more information about the project.

8. What they (of-er-ed) was unacceptable.

9. How will the new plan (ben-fit) the organization?

10. Another study is an (un-ec-es-ary) way to spend money.

(Answers on page 8)

ANSWERS TO EXERCISE #1

1. consistent

2. capitol

3. extension

4. separate

5. supersede

6. preceding

7. occurred

8. offered

9. benefit

10. unnecessary

EXERCISE #2—SPELLING SHORTCUTS

Following are three handy shortcuts to improve your spelling. (1) If a word gives you trouble, deliberately mispronounce it, emphasizing the troublesome part of the word. To fix the spelling of words such as *separate* and *benefit* in your mind, say ''sep-<u>ay</u>-rate,'' ''ben-<u>ee</u>-fit.'' (2) Look for little words in big words. Noticing the word *iron* in *environment* can help you remember the longer, more difficult word. (3) Use gimmicks to fix the spelling of difficult words in your mind. For example, ''Many capit<u>o</u>l buildings have an 'o' shaped dome.''

Correctly spell the words listed below. Use the memory devices suggested on the next page (or make up your own) for any words you misspell.

1. cred-bility _____

2. extr-m-ly _____

3. occur-ed _____

4. expl-nation _____

5. pron-nciation _____

6. cat-gory _____

7. priv-l-ge _____

8. gasol-ne _____

9. super-ede (*s* or *c?*) _____

10. contr-versial _____

(Answers on page 10)

ANSWERS TO EXERCISE #2

1. credibility   I hope I have credibility.

2. extremely   ex-trem-e-ly (pronunciation)

3. occurred   The accident occurred on the railroad tracks.

4. explanation   explanation

5. pronunciation   pronunciation

6. category   cat-e-gory (pronunciation)

7. privilege   privilege

8. gasoline   gasoline

9. supersede   The word "supersede" has two s's.

10. controversial   Oh, so controversial!

EXERCISE #3—SPELLING RULES

How are you on spelling rules? Here's a quick review of four important ones. In the sentences below, spell the bracketed word correctly if you can, then check your answers (and which rule applies), on the next page.

1. We hope to (rec-ve) the shipment this week.

2. The new tariff will hurt our (for-gn) competitors.

3. The (financ-r) was charged with tax evasion.

4. Nothing is sure but death and (tax-).

5. His skill in diplomacy makes friends out of (enem-s).

6. Are you (accus-ng) the Japanese of chip-dumping?

7. In my (judg-ent), profits will be up significantly in April.

8. Be sure to include a (sum-ry) at the end of your report.

9. Some companies have (benefit-d) from the drop in the dollar's value.

10. Mr. Wombat has been (transfer-d) to Minot, N.D.

(Answers on page 12)

ANSWERS TO EXERCISE #3

1. receive   The rule is i before e, except after c.

2. foreign   It's i before e or ei after the letter c if the sound of the two letters combined is ''ee''; if not, the pattern is reversed.

3. financier   Every rule has a few exceptions. Other examples are either, neither, seize, leisure, weird, sheik.

4. taxes   Add s to form the plurals of most nouns; if the noun ends in an ''s'' sound, add es. Add es also to some nouns ending in o. (tomatoes, potatoes, vetoes, torpedoes).

5. enemies   If a noun ends in y preceded by a consonant, change the y to i and add es. If a noun ends in y preceded by a vowel, simply add s to form the plural. Exception: proper nouns. The plural of Kennedy is Kennedys.

6. accusing   Drop the final silent e when adding suffixes that begin with a vowel (accuse + ing). Keep the final silent e when adding suffixes that begin with a consonant (hope + less = hopeless).

7. judgment   Exception. Some others are courageous, dyeing, argument, and truly.

8. summary   Double the final consonant when adding a suffix that begins with a vowel if the consonant is preceded by a single vowel (sum + ary).

9. benefited   With words of two or more syllables, double the final consonant only if the accent is on the last syllable.

10. transferred   An exception. Since the preferred pronunciation is with the accent on the first syllable (trans'fer), you would not expect the final consonant to be doubled. Other exceptions are transferring excellent, excellence.

EXERCISE #4—THE APOSTROPHE

Test your knowledge of the proper use of apostrophes by circling errors in the sentences below. The apostrophe (') is used to show possession or ownership, or to mark an omission. Correctly punctuated sentences and the rules that apply are found on the next page.

1. The office managers new rule was unpopular with the secretaries.

2. The secretarys chair was adjusted by the manager's assistant.

3. Charles cap was the same color as his boss's face.

4. The managers smiled when they read the salesmens' reports.

5. Both speaker's comments were greeted with applause.

6. Anyones guess is as good as mine.

7. Their report was more optimistic than our's.

8. It doesn't matter; its not our concern.

9. The accountant's will meet with the manager's on Friday.

10. She often forgets to dot her is.

(Answers on page 14)

ANSWERS TO EXERCISE #4

1. The office (manager's) new rule was unpopular with the secretaries.

    Rule: *All singular nouns use apostrophe and s to show possession or ownership.*

2. The (secretary's) chair was adjusted by the manager's assistant.

    Rule: *Same as above.*

3. (Charles's) cap was the same color as his boss's face.

    Rule: *ALL singular nouns, including those ending in s like Charles and boss, use apostrophe and s to show possession or ownership.*

4. The managers smiled when they read the (salesmen's) reports.

    Rule: *Plural nouns that do not end in s use apostrophe and s to show possession or ownership.*

5. Both (speakers') comments were greeted with applause.

    Rule: *Plural nouns that end in s (most plurals do) take only an apostrophe to show possession or ownership.*

6. (Anyone's) guess is as good as mine.

    Rule: *Indefinite pronouns (one, anyone, everyone, someone, anybody, everybody, nobody, another) show possession just like singular nouns: by adding apostrophe and s.*

7. Their report was more optimistic than (ours.)

    Rule: *Personal pronouns (hers, his, its, ours, yours, theirs) do not take an apostrophe to show possession.*

8. It doesn't matter; (it's) not our concern.

    Rule: *Contractions require apostrophes to show omitted letters. BE SURE TO NOTE THE PLACEMENT OF THE APOSTROPHE.*

9. The (accountants) will meet with the (managers) on Friday.

    Rule: *Do not use an apostrophe to indicate a plural noun. DO NOT CONFUSE POSSESSIVES AND PLURALS.*

10. She often forgets to dot her (i's.)

    Rule: *Do not use an apostrophe to indicate a plural noun unless it would be confusing without one.*

EXERCISE #5—THE COMMA

To use a comma or not to use a comma, that is the question. The comma is a signal indicating a needed pause within a sentence. Add needed commas to the sentences below. Strike out or change punctuation that is unnecessary or incorrect.

1. The reason is, we weren't sure about the meeting date, when I called.

2. Section Chief, Bill Jones, will meet with us Friday.

3. Next year's conference will be in Denver, I hope to see you there.

4. The accountants gave us the good news and then they sent us their bill.

5. I have not completed my report so I cannot answer your question.

6. The boss likes scotch bourbon and beer.

7. He is a clever efficient manager.

8. Mr. Johnson, who gave the incorrect figure to the IRS will lead us in a moment of silent prayer.

9. The error, that Mr. Fleegle discovered, was not a serious one.

10. ''We are going to meet our deadline'' the manager said.

(Answers on page 16)

ANSWERS TO EXERCISE #5

1. The reason is we weren't sure about the meeting date when I called.
   Rule: *Don't overuse commas. ''When in doubt, leave it out.''*

2. Section Chief Bill Jones will meet with us Friday.
   Rule: *Same as above.*

3. Next year's conference will be in Denver; I hope to see you there.
   Rule: *Don't link complete sentences with a comma; use a semicolon instead. NOTE: A COMMA IS A SIGNAL MEANING ''PAUSE.'' A SEMICOLON, LIKE A PERIOD, MEANS ''STOP.''*

4. The accountants gave us the good news, and then they sent us their bill.
   Rule: *Use a comma before linking words (coordinating conjunctions) such as and, but, or, for, yet, so.*

5. I have not completed my report, so I cannot answer your question.
   Rule: *Same as above.*

6. The boss likes scotch, bourbon, and beer.
   Rule: *Separate items in a series with commas. NOTE: ADD THE ''SERIAL COMMA'' (THE LAST ONE) TO AVOID CONFUSION.*

7. He is a clever, efficient manager.
   Rule: *Place a comma between adjectives of equal importance.*

8. Mr. Johnson, who gave the incorrect figure to the IRS, will lead us in a moment of silent prayer.
   Rule: *Do not omit the second comma from comma pairs.*

9. The error that Mr. Fleegle discovered was not a serious one.
   Rule: *Use a comma before ''which,'' not before ''that.'' NOTE: CHANGING WHICH TO THAT CHANGES THE MEANING OF THE SENTENCE.*

10. ''We are going to meet our deadline,'' the manager said.
    Rule: *Use a comma to separate a direct quotation from explanatory words.*

EXERCISE #6—CAPITAL LETTERS

Let's see how much you know about capitalization. Capital letters are used with surnames, days of the week, months, holidays, titles before a name, specific place names, and important words in titles. In the sentences below, add or subtract capital letters as needed.

1. Last year the meeting was held on a wednesday in June, or maybe it was later in the Summer.

2. Do we cross the Truckee river before we get to the lake?

3. I understand that Captain Johnson will speak first and then the Senator.

4. The boss has a picture of his Mother on his desk.

5. The new salesman is a republican, a Catholic, and he speaks fluent Norwegian and chinese.

6. Drive South six blocks; you will see the Chrysler building on your left.

7. He is taking accounting and english at a local junior college.

8. He is also taking history and health education 1a.

9. His favorite novel is *The Catcher In The Rye*.

10. Our high school will hold its ten year reunion next month.

(Answers on page 18)

ANSWERS TO EXERCISE #6.

1. Last year the meeting was held on a Wednesday in June, or maybe it was later in the summer.
    Rule: *Capitalize the names of days of the week, months, but not seasons.*

2. Do we cross the Truckee River before we get to the lake?
    Rule: *Capitalize the specific names of places.*

3. I understand that Captain Johnson will speak first and then the senator.
    Rule: *Capitalize titles in front of names, not otherwise.*

4. The boss has a picture of his mother on his desk.
    Rule: *Capitalize ''mother'' and ''father'' when they are used as names, not when they follow words like my, our, his, etc.*

5. The new salesman is a Republican, a Catholic, and he speaks fluent Norwegian and Chinese.
    Rule: *Capitalize the names of political parties, religions, and languages.*

6. Drive south six blocks; you will see the Chrysler Building on your left.
    Rule: *Capitalize the names of regions, but not directions. Capitalize the names of buildings.*

7. He is taking accounting and English at a local junior college.
    Rule: *Do not capitalize the names of general study areas. In this case, capitalize ''English'' because it is also the name of a language.*

8. He is also taking history and Health Education 1A.
    Rule: *Do not capitalize the names of general study areas. Do capitalize specific course titles.*

9. His favorite novel is *The Catcher in the Rye*.
    Rule: *Capitalize the first word of a title. Otherwise do not capitalize articles (a, an, the), short prepositions (of, on, with, etc.), and conjunctions (and, but, or, etc.).*

10. Our high school will hold its ten-year reunion next month.
    Rule: *Capitalize only the specific names of places, e.g. ''Woodside High School.''*

EXERCISE #7—MECHANICS

Here's a test of your knowledge of mechanics. In the sentences below, find and correct any mistakes in placement of punctuation marks, use of quotation marks and italics, use of numbers, abbreviations, etc.

1. Patrick Henry said, ''Give me liberty or give me death''.

2. He said his plans are ''uncertain at this time;'' he promised to make up his mind by next week.

3. President Kennedy said, 'Ask not what your country can do for you.'

4. My favorite short story is <u>The Most Dangerous Game</u>.

5. Every morning I read the ''Wall Street Journal.''

6. We are expecting 200 guests for the reception on the 33rd floor of the hotel.

7. They received one-hundred and thirty-eight calls in response to the ad.

8. She reported that sales were up seven percent last month.

9. The chairman earned $1 million last year.

10. There are many valuable spelling rules, i.e. the rule governing the formation of plurals.

(Answers on page 20)

ANSWERS TO EXERCISE #7

1. Patrick Henry said, ''Give me liberty or give me death.''
    Rule: *Place commas and periods inside quotation marks.*

2. He said his plans are ''uncertain at this time''; he promised to make up his mind by next week.
    Rule: *Place colons and semicolons outside quotation marks.*

3. President Kennedy said, ''Ask not what your country can do for you.''
    Rule: *Use single quotation marks (') only for quotations within quotations.*

4. My favorite short story is ''The Most Dangerous Game.''
    Rule: *Use quotation marks for titles of printed materials that are not book length (stories, poems, articles, etc.).*

5. Every morning I read the *Wall Street Journal*.
    Rule: *Use italics (underline) for titles of books, magazines, newspapers, etc..*

6. We are expecting two hundred guests for the reception on the thirty-third floor of the hotel.
    Rule: *Write out a number in words when it will take only one or two words.*

7. They received 138 calls in response to the ad.
    Rule: *Use figures for any number that would be three or more words when written out.*

8. She reported that sales were up 7% last month.
    Rule: *Use figures for percentages. Also for dates; addresses; room numbers; telephone numbers; chapter, page, and line numbers; serial numbers; decimals; route numbers; times; statistics; and precise measurements.*

9. The chairman earned a million dollars last year.
    Rule: *Write amounts of money as follows: a million dollars, $6 million, $6,847,211.*

10. There are many valuable spelling rules, e.g., the rule governing the formation of plurals.
    Rule: *I.e. means ''that is''; e.g. means ''for example.''*

EXERCISE #8—USAGE

And now for some of the finer points. Even advanced students may find this usage quiz challenging. Good luck!

1. Which is correct? (a) scholar-athlete, (b) wildly-successful debut.

_____

2. Which is correct? (a) 19 BC, (b) AD 565.

_____

3. Do you underline, or place in quotation marks, the names of: films, TV programs, paintings, ships, song titles, episodes of a TV program?

_____

4. Which of the following should be underlined, which put in quotes? Bible, Genesis, Koran.

_____

5. When you are _absolutely certain_, do you say ''doubtless,'' ''no doubt,'' or ''undoubtedly''?

_____

6. Find the error in the following statement (from a speech by Sen. Edward Kennedy): ''If I was to make a political decision, it would be a different announcement today.''

_____

7. Which of these advertising slogans is incorrect grammatically? (a) ''Us Tareyton smokers would rather fight than switch.'' (b) ''For we full-figured gals.''

_____

8. Which is correct? (a) high school teacher, (b) camel's hair brush, (c) small businessman.

_____

9. Which is correct? (a) in regards to, (b) as regards, (c) in regard to.

_____

10. Which spelling is correct in each of the following word pairs? (a) all ready/already, (b) all right/alright, (c) a lot/alot.

_____

(Answers on page 22)

ANSWERS TO EXERCISE #8

1. (a) is correct. Hyphenate pairs of coequal nouns. Adverbs ending in <u>ly</u> do not form hyphenated compounds.

2. Both are correct.

3. Underline the first four; use quotes for the last two.

4. None. The rule for marking book titles and chapters does not apply to sacred writing.

5. Undoubtedly.

6. "If I <u>were</u>..." <u>Was</u> becomes <u>were</u> in the subjunctive mood. The subjunctive mood expresses doubt, uncertainty, wish, or supposition or signals a condition contrary to fact.

7. Both are incorrect. It should be "<u>We</u> Tareyton smokers..." and "For <u>us</u> full-figured gals."

8. All could be correct, but not unless you mean "teacher on drugs," "well-groomed camel," or "short businessman." Write (a) high-school teacher, (b) camel's-hair brush, (c) small-business man if you have another meaning in mind.

9. (b) and (c) are correct.

10. (a) Both are correct. (b) All right. (c) A lot.

PART III— STARTING WITH THE SENTENCE

STARTING WITH THE SENTENCE

Clear Sentences

Perhaps your basic skills are fundamentally sound. You can spell most words, know how to punctuate and make few grammatical mistakes. If this is the case, the next step in building a better writing style is to concentrate on improving your sentences. A good English sentence is economical, simple, and clear. A sentence should contain no unnecessary words. It should consist of simple, familiar words. The business writer's main enemies are passive sentences, too many words, overuse of big words, and cliches. In this section you will practice changing weak passive sentences to ones that are active. You will trim unneeded words from sentences and learn to substitute familiar words for jargon and abstractions. You will translate pompous, complex, and hard to read prose into plain English. You will also learn to avoid some common business writing cliches such as "enclosed please find." Finally, you will do a simple proofreading exercise which will remind you to watch out for careless errors.

Principles of Effective Style

You can learn to write better by putting into practice a few simple principles of effective style. You may have to break some bad habits in the process, but that shouldn't be too difficult. Following are some basic rules:

1. When you finish a draft of a memo or letter, reread it carefully and trim unnecessary words.

2. Simplify your language. Don't try to impress a reader with your vocabulary.

3. Scan your writing for passive sentences and standard business phrases. Make passive sentences active by changing the positions of subject and verb, and remove all cliches.

4. Proofread your memo or letter carefully and correct any errors in spelling, typing, etc.. Aim for a final draft that *looks* good as well as clearly communicates your message.

EXERCISE #9—ACTIVE VERSUS PASSIVE SENTENCES

Following is a formula for more readable writing. Use simple, active sentences made up of familiar, concrete words. First, write with active sentences. In an active sentence, the *doer* of an action is named first, *before* the verb. In a passive sentence the doer (if mentioned at all) appears in a phrase *after* the verb: ''The meeting was changed <u>by the sales manager</u>.'' Change each of the sentences below from passive to active.

Passive: <u>The meeting was called to order by Ted.</u>

Active: <u>Ted called the meeting to order.</u>

Plans for the conference will be made by the staff assistant.

_____

An error has been discovered by our staff.

_____

The report will be reviewed by us.

_____

A decision was made to terminate the search.

_____

The mistake in billing will be rectified by the supplier posthaste.

_____

Receipt of your letter is acknowledged and appreciated.

_____

Cost-cutting procedures are advised by the vice-president.

_____

(Answers on page 26)

ANSWERS TO EXERCISE #9

Plans for the conference will be made by the staff assistant.

The staff assistant will plan the conference.

An error has been discovered by our staff.

Our staff has discovered an error.

The report will be reviewed by us.

We will review the report.

A decision was made to terminate the search.

We decided to stop looking.

The mistake in billing will be rectified by the supplier posthaste.

The supplier will correct the billing mistake immediately.

Receipt of your letter is acknowledged and appreciated.

Thank you for your letter.

Cost-cutting procedures are advised by the vice-president.

The vice-president says we have to cut costs.

EXERCISE #10—USE FAMILIAR WORDS

To be sure that your meaning will be clear to all readers, use familiar words. Substitute shorter, simpler words for each of the words listed below. If you do not know the meaning of any word on the list, refer to your dictionary.

assemblage	crowd
metropolis	city
visage	
utilize	
initial	
facilitate	
ascertain	
initiate	
optimum	
entities	
presently	
disseminate	
commence	
illumination	
extinguish	
terminate	

(Answers on page 28)

ANSWERS TO EXERCISE #10

assemblage	crowd
metropolis	city
visage	face
utilize	use
initial	first
facilitate	ease, aid
ascertain	find out
initiate	start
optimum	best
entities	things
presently	soon
disseminate	spread
commence	begin, start
illumination	lights
extinguish	turn out
terminate	end

EXERCISE #11—ELIMINATE UNNECESSARY WORDS

"Too many words" is a common fault of bad writing. Improve each of the following sentences by penciling out unnecessary words. Reword the sentence if needed.

1. Somebody has said that words are a lot like inflated money—the more of them that you use, the less each one of them is worth.

2. I was unaware of the fact that your widget could be used for security purposes.

3. Mr. Jones, who is a member of the same firm, put the report together in a hasty manner.

4. The reason why we failed to reply is that we were not apprised of the fact until yesterday that somehow the report had been unavoidably delayed.

5. The fact that he had not succeeded was brought to my attention recently.

6. The degree of importance in the level of accuracy depends upon the individual situations.

(Answers on page 30)

1. Somebody has said that words are ~~a lot~~ like inflated money—the more ~~of them that~~ you use, the less each ~~one of them~~ is worth.

2. I was unaware ~~of the fac~~t that your widget could be used for security ~~purposes.~~

3. Mr. Jones, ~~who is~~ a member of the same firm, put the report together ~~in a~~ hast*il*y ~~manner~~.

4. ~~The reason why we failed to~~ *We didn't* reply, ~~is that~~ we ~~were not apprised of the fact~~ *because learned only* ~~until~~ yesterday that ~~somehow~~ the report had been ~~unavoidably~~ delayed.

5. ~~The fact that he had not succeeded was brought to my attention~~ *I learned he failed.* recently.

6. The ~~degree of~~ importance ~~in the level~~ of accuracy depends upon the ~~individual~~ situation~~s~~.

EXERCISE #12—MORE ON WASTED WORDS

The most common word-wasters are "windy phrases." How would you shorten the phrases listed below?

at the present time	now
in the event of	if
in the majority of instances	
in spite of the fact that	
in view of the fact that	
there is no doubt but that	
owing to the fact that	
in my opinion, I think	
each and everyone	
of a hostile nature	
in short supply	
make contact with	
made the statement that	
by the withdrawing of	

(Answers on page 32)

ANSWERS TO EXERCISE #12

at the present time	now
in the event of	if
in the majority of instances	usually
in spite of the fact that	although
in view of the fact that	because
there is no doubt but that	undoubtedly
owing to the fact that	since
in my opinion, I think	(omit)
each and everyone	each one
of a hostile nature	hostile
in short supply	scarce
make contact with	contact
made the statement that	stated, said
by the withdrawing of	by withdrawing

EXERCISE #13—AVOID REDUNDANCY

Another type of wordiness is caused by redundant expressions. In the word pairs listed below, which of the words can be omitted?

~~close~~ proximity

clenched ~~tightly~~

refer back

continue on

definite decision

circle around

absolutely essential

rather unique

advance planning

and moreover

basic fundamentals

blend together

brief moment

but nevertheless

(Answers on page 34)

34

ANSWERS TO EXERCISE #13

~~close~~ proximity

clenched ~~tightly~~

refer ~~back~~

continue ~~on~~

~~definite~~ decision

circle ~~around~~

~~absolutely~~ essential

~~rather~~ unique

~~advance~~ planning

~~and~~ moreover

~~basic~~ fundamentals

blend ~~together~~

~~brief~~ moment

~~but~~ nevertheless

EXERCISE #14—USE ADJECTIVES SPARINGLY

Another kind of wordiness results from too many adjectives and adverbs. Use adjectives and adverbs sparingly. Often helping words are unnecessary if the writer chooses his words carefully. In the examples below, replace each verb or noun with a more specific word and omit adjectives and adverbs.

pursue vigorously	strive
powerful increase	
move swiftly	
erroneous decision	
moved moderately higher	
decline sharply	
moved rapidly higher	
exert irresistable pressure	
preliminary investigation	
halted suddenly and completely	

(Answers on page 36)

36

pursue vigorously	strive
powerful increase	surge
move swiftly	hurry
erroneous decision	mistake
moved moderately higher	rose
decline sharply	plummet
moved rapidly higher	soared
exert irresistable pressure	force
preliminary investigation	probe
halted suddenly and completely	blocked

EXERCISE #15—SHORT WORDS ARE BETTER

The following phrases and sentences are unclear (and silly) because the writers have used too many big words. Try to figure out the intended meaning in each example.

Illumination is required to be extinguished on these premises after nightfall.

   Lights out after dark.
_____

My thinking has evolved to the significant point where a concept has emerged.

_____

I acknowledge receipt of your letter and I beg to thank you.

_____

Subsequently we will require your endorsement.

_____

The biota exhibited a one-hundred percent mortality rate.

_____

We are endeavoring to construct a more inclusive society.

_____

At this juncture of maturization.

_____

Communication is the imparting of meaningful informational modes or concepts that impact on interpersonal inputs and interfacings.

_____

(Answers on page 38)

38

Illumination is required to be extinguished on these premises after nightfall.

Lights out after dark.

My thinking has evolved to the significant point where a concept has emerged.

I had an idea.

I acknowledge receipt of your letter and I beg to thank you.

Thank you for the letter.

Subsequently we will require your endorsement.

Later we will need your signature.

The biota exhibited a one-hundred percent mortality rate.

All the fish died.

We are endeavoring to construct a more inclusive society.

We are going to make a country in which no one is left out.

At this juncture of maturization.

Now.

Communication is the imparting of meaningful informational modes or concepts that impact on interpersonal inputs and interfacings.

?

EXERCISE #16—AVOID CLICHES

Try to find fresh words to express your ideas. Here is a list of common business cliches. Rewrite *three* of them (your choice) using simpler, clearer, better language.

enclosed please find

please be advised that

at your earliest convenience

acknowledge receipt of

in reference to the above-named subject matter

hoping to hear from you, I remain

as per our conversation

we are returning same herewith

regarding the matter of

it has come to our attention.

1. _____

2. _____

3. _____

(Answers on page 40)

ANSWERS TO EXERCISE #16

enclosed please find   *I am enclosing, we are enclosing*

please be advised that   *(omit)*

at your earliest convenience   *soon, by Friday*

acknowledge receipt of   *received*

in reference to the above-named subject matter   *(omit)*

hoping to hear from you, I remain   *(omit)*

as per our conversation   *as you said*

we are returning same herewith   *we are returning (name item)*

regarding the matter of   *(omit)*

it has come to our attention.   *We have discussed, learned*

EXERCISE #17—PAY ATTENTION TO DETAIL

Pay attention to detail! Don't ignore the little things. Your letters and memos should look good and be free of errors. Find and circle "typos" and other errors (grammar, spelling, punctuation, mechanics) in the sentences below.

1. Thank you for your interest in our firm, this letter will summarize the services we can provide for you.

2. Many of our clients are doctors. With practices similar to yours.

3. We can provide a complete financial analysis to determine if its beneficial to incorporate your practice.

4. Our accountant's are currently examining the figures you sent us.

5. We are looking forward to meeting with you later this fall.

6. We have scheduled a conference for next month and these figures will be discussed at that time.

7. I am sure that we can accomodate your request.

8. A meeting will be held on Friday, 18 July, at 3 p.m., in the regional managers office.

9. Unfortunately I cannot supply the figures which you requested.

10. I'm happy to hear your Pomeranian, Puffy was pleased with the new pet spa on the West Side.

11. What we are offering you is a very unique investment opportunity.

12. Obviously, alot of time and effort went into your report.

13. Mr. Smith commented that it would be "unwise to take action at this time".

14. Enclosed please find my resume and supporting in response to your advertised need for a Communications Coordinator.

15. Your information is consistant with our findings.

(Answers on page 42)

42

1. Thank you for your interest in our firm this letter will summarize the   ;
   services we can provide for you.

2. Many of our clients are doctors With practices similar to yours.   , *with*

3. We can provide a complete financial analysis to determine if its beneficial to   *it's*
   incorporate your practice.

4. Our accountant's are currently examining the figures you sent us.   *ts*

5. We are looking forward to meeting with you later this fall.   *ok*

6. We have scheduled a conference for next month and these figures will be   , *and*
   discussed at that time.

7. I am sure that we can accomodate your request.   *mm*

8. A meeting will be held on Friday, 18 July, at 3 p.m., in the regional managers   *r's*
   office.

9. Unfortunately I cannot supply the figures which you requested.   *that*

10. I'm happy to hear your Pomeranian, Puffy was pleased with the new pet spa   ,
    on the West Side.

11. What we are offering you is a very unique investment opportunity.   *(omit)*

12. Obviously, alot of time and effort went into your report.   *a lot*

13. Mr. Smith commented that it would be "unwise to take action at this time".   . "

14. Enclosed please find my resume and supporting in response to your   *missing word*
    advertised need for a Communications Coordinator.

15. Your information is consistant with our findings.   *ent*

EXERCISE #18—MISPLACED WORDS

Choose your words carefully. Also pay attention to the placement of words and phrases in your sentences. Revise the sentences below. Help the writers say what they mean!

Please give the desk to Ms. Benson with the thin legs.

_____

When he went to investigate the claim, a dog bit Mr. Frisbee.

_____

Never buy envelopes from a dealer without a gummed flap.

_____

Mr. Tuggle with the 2K memory will be testing the new machine.

_____

The car is parked behind the office which is out of gas.

_____

The calculator is in Mr. Newell's office which doesn't work.

_____

Down in January again, the manager was displeased with the sales figures.

_____

Acme houses provide comfort for people with central air conditioning and heating.

_____

_____

(Answers on page 44)

ANSWERS TO EXERCISE #18

Please give the desk to Ms. Benson with the thin legs.

Please give the desk with the thin legs to Ms. Benson.

When he went to investigate the claim, a dog bit Mr. Frisbee.

When Mr. Frisbee went to investigate the claim, a dog bit him.

Never buy envelopes from a dealer without a gummed flap.

Never buy envelopes without a gummed flap from a dealer.

Mr. Tuggle with the 2K memory will be testing the new machine.

Mr. Tuggle will be testing the new machine with the 2K memory.

The car is parked behind the office which is out of gas.

The car, which is out of gas, is parked behind the office.

The calculator is in Mr. Newell's office which doesn't work.

The calculator, which doesn't work, is in Mr. Newell's office.

Down in January again, the manager was displeased with the sales figures.

The manager was displeased with the sales figures which were down again in January.

Acme houses provide comfort for people with central air conditioning and heating.

Acme houses with central air conditioning and heating provide comfort for people.

EXERCISE #19—WEAKLING VERBS

Weakling verbs don't belong in your letters and memos. Get rid of them. Replace them with verbs with muscle. Look for words that describe actions all by themselves, without helping words or phrases. Below, replace (don't "find replacments for") the weak verbs listed.

WEAK	STRONG
make substitution	substitute
have intention	intend
become an imposition	
was becoming	
had not succeeded	
call your attention to	
compells me to conclude	
face up to	
gave assistance to	
gave an explanation	
responsible for supervision of	
conducted an inspection of	
did the marketing for	

(Answers on page 46)

46

WEAK	STRONG
make substitution	substitute
have intention	intend
become an imposition	impose
was becoming	became
had not succeeded	failed
call your attention to	remind, notify
compells me to conclude	I realize
face up to	face
gave assistance to	assisted
gave an explanation	explained
responsible for supervision of	supervised
conducted an inspection of	inspected
did the marketing for	marketed

PART IV— EXERCISES TO HELP YOU WRITE BETTER MEMOS

EXERCISES TO HELP YOU WRITE BETTER MEMOS

Clear, Direct, and Concise

A good memo can inform, persuade, and impress your reader. It can save your organization both time and money. If nothing else, learning to write a better memo will save *you* time and effort. It is unproductive to struggle for thirty minutes over the wording of a paragraph that should take five minutes to write.

A good memo should be clear, direct, and concise. The most important thought should be at the beginning of the memo. Directives and requests should be specific. (*"Please call me on Monday"* rather than *"Get back to me as soon as possible."*) The language of a memo should be plain, simple English. If a memo sounds dull and stiff, rewrite it using language that is more conversational. (*Reading a memo aloud will help you detect pompous language and unnecessary words.*)

Set Off Important Points

A good trick is to *highlight* important points by putting them in separate paragraphs or by using numbers, letters, or bullets to set them off. Like this:

- Keep memos to one page maximum. No exceptions.

- Keep sentences short. Under fifteen words is a good rule of thumb.

- Proofread the memo when you finish. Correct inconsistencies in format, spelling errors, words that need capitalization.

Sample Memos

The sample memos in this chapter are for you to compare and revise. First study the memos on page 49. Compare the samples and read the analysis of strengths and weaknesses that follow. Then begin the exercises which ask you to revise memos. In each case, make whatever changes are necessary to improve the wording and format of the sample.

Memo #1

Pursuant to phone contact of October 7, final sales totals for the quarter ending in September are enclosed herewith. A planning conference for all sales personnel will be scheduled for the near future and these figures will be discussed. It is hoped that all district managers will be aware that the figures are such that reductions in the total number of dealerships and retail units may be indicated. A meeting to discuss this matter will be held on Monday, 17 October, at 10 a.m., in the regional manager's office. Thank you for your cooperation.

Analysis. This memo is grammatical and free of errors in spelling and mechanics. But the wordy style and passive voice make the memo difficult to read and understand. What is the message? Essentially, that sales are off, inventories are too high, and the company may cut some dealerships soon. Perhaps the writer was uncomfortable about communicating bad news, or perhaps he or she mistakenly thinks business writing is supposed to sound this way. Whatever the reason, this memo gets low marks for readability. It is stuffy, roundabout, and impersonal. Specific writing faults are passive sentences, wordy expressions, and cliches.

Memo #2

I have read your letter regarding your request for transfer. Travel time to work and a lack of hours are strong reasons for transfer. Presently A & Z can't offer you any position in the San Francisco area. I relize you are eager to transfer, but, there are no positions for which you qualify. If a position becomes available you will be strongly considered. Continue to perform as excellently as you have in the past. Togather we can find a solution to this problem. Feel free to reapply for transfer in six months. I am sorry we were unable to comply with your request. If you have any questions give me a call at 643-7582.

Analysis. This memo is direct, concise, and basically clear. Unfortunately, it is weak mechanically. Missing words, punctuation errors, and several misspellings spoil the memo. Undoubtedly the writer meant to say that there are no *available* positions for which the employee qualifies. The phrase ''a lack of hours'' is unclear. Breaking the memo into two paragraphs would help improve its appearance. Also, the memo sounds choppy; the writer could achieve better sentence variety by combining several short sentences.

50

> ### Memo #3

I spoke with the Data Processing Department about your transfer. There are no positions available for a person with your qualifications. The minimum qualifications for a position in Data Processing are an A.A. degree in computer science and one year of programing experience.

If you wish to complete the necessary education, you may wish to consider taking advantage of our company's tuition program. I can adjust your work schedule to give you time to complete your education. Please let me know if you want to take advantage of this opportunity.

If you have questions or would like to discuss your transfer, please call me.

Analysis. This memo is clear, direct and supportive. The author balances bad news with helpful suggestions and alternatives. Notice especially how the writing *sounds*. The prose is simple, natural, clear: plain English at its best.

EXERCISE #20—REVISING A MEMO (1)

Revise the memo below. The original sounds stiff and cold; rewrite it using language that is more personal and human. Change passive sentences to active. Also correct errors in spelling and punctuation.

TO: All employees

FROM: Carol Smith/Human Resources

SUBJECT: Cancellation of July 4th's picnic

DATE: May 27, 1986

It is with great regret that the July 4th's picnic at Central Park has been cancelled.   Due to our present reorganization, President John K. Hoff and other senior management have decided that Liberty Savings & Loan Association could not financially justify such an event at this time.

Since these events are so important for the morale of the company, management is hoping to be in a better position to provide its employees with a well deserved Christmas party.   And with everyone's help, management knows we will be able to celebrate the holidays like never before.

Mr. Hoff thanks you for making this great sacrafice during Liberty's hard times,   In making these types of sacrafices, you are helping to ensure a better future for all. Watch for exciting news regarding this year's Christmas party in Liberty's monthly news letter, you can make it happen.

(Corrected versions on page 52)

52

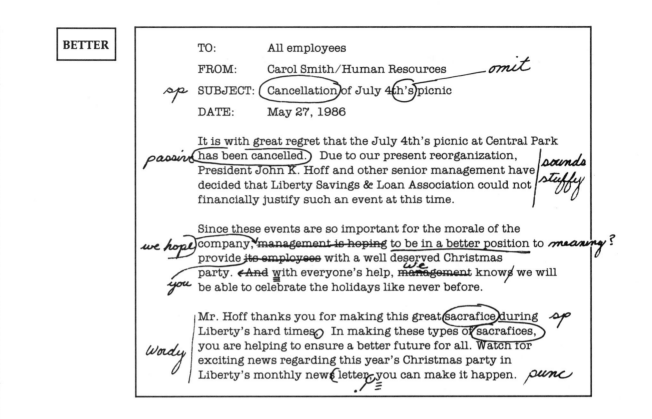

BETTER

TO: All employees

FROM: Carol Smith/Human Resources   *omit*

sp   SUBJECT: ⟨Cancellation⟩ of July 4⟨th's⟩ picnic

DATE: May 27, 1986

It is with great regret that the July 4th's picnic at Central Park

passive ⟨has been cancelled.⟩ Due to our present reorganization,   *sounds*
President John K. Hoff and other senior management have   *stuffy*
decided that Liberty Savings & Loan Association could not
financially justify such an event at this time.

Since these events are so important for the morale of the
we hope company, ~~management is hoping~~ to be in a better position to *meaning?*
provide ~~its employees~~ with a well deserved Christmas
                                              we
party. ~~And~~ with everyone's help, ~~management~~ knows we will
you be able to celebrate the holidays like never before.

Mr. Hoff thanks you for making this great ⟨sacrafice⟩ during *sp*
Liberty's hard times○ In making these types of ⟨sacrafices,⟩
Wordy you are helping to ensure a better future for all. Watch for
exciting news regarding this year's Christmas party in
Liberty's monthly news letter○ you can make it happen. *punc*

BEST

TO: All employees

FROM: Carol Smith/Human Resources

SUBJECT: Cancelation of July 4 picnic

DATE: May 27, 1986

I am sorry to inform you that the July 4 picnic at Central park
is canceled. Because of our recent reorganization, President Hoff
has decided Liberty Savings cannot financially justify a picnic.

Because special events are important for the morale of the
company, we plan to provide you with a well-deserved
Christmas party. With everyone's help, we should be able to
celebrate the holidays like never before.

Mr. Hoff thanks you for making this sacrifice and appreciates
your understanding to ensure a better future for Liberty Savings.

EXERCISE #21—REVISING A MEMO (2)

Revise the memo below. The memo's number one fault is *wordiness*. Get out your blue pencil and cross out unnecessary words and sentences. Also, substitute familiar words for big words. Make the tone of the memo more conversational.

POOR

TO: All employees

FROM: Randy Plunkett, Director

DATE: October 3, 1986

RE: Contributions

It has recently been brought to my attention that only a small percentage of employees are contributors to the Family Relief Fund supported by the Personnel Department. This fund is the source of money for the alleviation of employee hardship and emergencies which happen from time to time to employees.

It is hoped by this management that encouragement and motivation will be offered by each of you in supporting this worthwhile endeavor. Unless the level of contributions reaches a significant increase soon, a decline will be apparent in the formerly strong contribution level of all employees.

It is understood that no employee or person should be forced to make a contribution to this fund. However, since we believe that a true belief in their community and a desire to see the problems of employees met face-to-face by workable solutions are shared by most employees of Bidwell & Sons, we are certain that undue or inappropriate persuasion techniques will not be needed by the management staff.

You may leave your contributions with Sandy in the Personnel Department office. Thank you for your generosity in supporting this valuable cause.

(Corrected versions on page 54)

BETTER

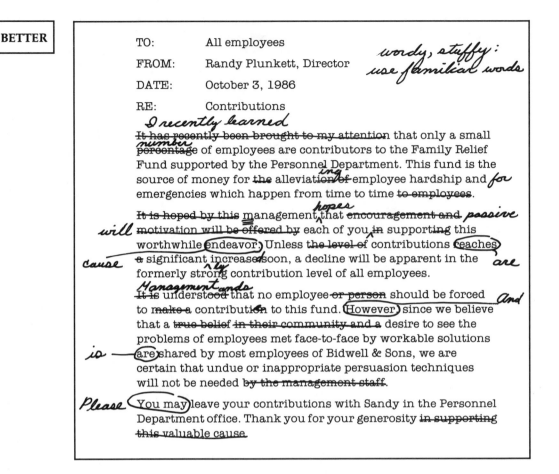

TO: All employees

FROM: Randy Plunkett, Director

DATE: October 3, 1986

RE: Contributions

wordy, stuffy: use familiar words

I recently learned
~~It has recently been brought to my attention~~ that only a small *number* ~~percentage~~ of employees are contributors to the Family Relief Fund supported by the Personnel Department. This fund is the source of money for ~~the~~ alleviation ~~of~~ employee hardship and *for* emergencies which happen from time to time ~~to employees~~.

hopes
~~It is hoped by this~~ management ~~that encouragement and~~ *passive* *will* ~~motivation will be offered by~~ each of you ~~in~~ supporting this worthwhile ⓔndeavor. Unless ~~the level of~~ contributions ⓡeaches *cause* ~~a~~ significant increase soon, a decline will be apparent in the *are* formerly strong contribution level of all employees.

Management ands
~~It is understood~~ that no employee ~~or person~~ should be forced *And* to ~~make a~~ contribution to this fund. ⓗowever since we believe that a ~~true belief in their community and a~~ desire to see the problems of employees met face-to-face by workable solutions *is* — ⓐre shared by most employees of Bidwell & Sons, we are certain that undue or inappropriate persuasion techniques will not be needed ~~by the management staff~~.

Please ⓨou may leave your contributions with Sandy in the Personnel Department office. Thank you for your generosity ~~in supporting this~~ valuable cause.

BEST

TO: All employees

FROM: Randy Plunkett, Director

DATE: October 3, 1986

RE: Contributions

I recently learned that only a small number of employees have contributed to the Family Relief Fund. This fund is supported by the Personnel Department and helps fellow employees meet emergencies.

I urge all of you to support this worthwhile cause. Management understands that no one should be forced to make a contribution to this fund. We also believe however that you would be willing to help a colleague achieve a workable solution to an emergency.

Please leave your contributions with Sandy in the Personnel Department office. Your generosity will be genuinely appreciated.

PART V—THE BUSINESS LETTER

THE BUSINESS LETTER

Write the Way You Talk

A business letter should be clear, direct, and businesslike. But it should also sound like it was written by a human being and not a machine. Business writing is often cold, stiff, and unnatural. Unthinking writers fall back on business cliches and passive sentences. They try to disguise uncertainty in a cloud of words. According to editor Malcolm Forbes, business writers should be positive, be nice, and be natural. Be natural—write the way you talk, says Forbes. This is good advice. Compare these two sentences:

NO: I acknowledge receipt of your letter and I beg to thank you.

YES: Thank you for your letter.

Consider the Reader

Another good piece of advice is to write a business letter from the point of view of the reader. Don't waste your readers' time with long, wordy letters. Edit ruthlessly. Cut every unnecessary word. On the other hand, make sure your readers don't have to puzzle over meaning. That's a timewaster, too. Add the facts, figures, and details needed to make the message clear.

NO: The recall affected their profits.

YES: Profits were down 10.4% the month following the recall.

Keep It Short

A good way to get a favorable response from a business letter is to keep it under one page in length. Keep paragraphs short, too. And make the letter *look* appealing. Type it on good quality bond paper, and make sure that there are no typos, misspellings, or factual errors on the copy that you send out.

Rewriting Letters

Part V contains several sample business letters that need editing and revision. Read each letter carefully. Look for sentences that should be reworded or shortened and for errors in spelling and mechanics. Make notes in the margins, if you like. Then rewrite the letter. Compare your finished letter with the revised version on the overleaf. Don't worry if your revision and the author's are not identical. One change is as good as another as long as the finished product is more readable.

A CHECKLIST FOR THE BUSINESS LETTER

- Tell what your letter is about in the first paragraph.

- If you're answering a letter, refer to the date it was written.

- Read your letter aloud when you are done to see if it sounds natural.

- Have a sense of humor, but don't be cute or flippant.

- Be specific.

- Use the active voice instead of the passive.

- Keep the letter short.

- For emphasis, <u>underline</u> important words.

- Make the final copy perfect.

- Don't exaggerate or try to pass off opinions as facts.

- Be clear and honest.

- Read the first draft of your letter and edit ruthlessly.

- In the final paragraph, tell the reader exactly what you want him or her to do, or what you are going to do. Don't omit this important ''action step.''

- Close with something simple like, ''Sincerely.''

EXERCISE #22—REVISING A BUSINESS LETTER (1)

Revise the job application letter reprinted below. Trim unnecessary words and rewrite awkward sentences. Note especially that this letter's author has been careless about details. Correct errors in grammar, punctuation, and mechanics.

(POOR)

Mr. William Frank
Personnel Director
ABC Design, Inc.
291 Front St.
San Francisco, Ca., 94128

   Dear Mr Frank;

Searching for an employee with qualifications to fit management or a position of responsibility with a degree in adversity. The job description you described in the *Western Placement Annual 1987*, is particularly suited to my qualifications. My previous positions in the federal government has provided me with skills to overcome problems and manifest myself as an achiever.

Mr. Frank, my graduation from Cal State University, Hayward Business Department, in June of '85, has provided me with skills along with my previous employment in government. Hearing your company has an opening in their Marketing and Sales department, I am applying for such a position. Knowing your company deals with a variety of products, I feel that my scope of knowledge of consumer wants and needs can widen your target market areas. My ability to work with the public and quickly locate their interests makes me a likely candidate.

The enclosed resume will clearly show my qualifications and abilities. Please read for yourself and be the judge.

In closing I would appreciate an interview at your convenience. Your company office is located near my home and I would like to meet with you at a time convenient for you. My home phone number after 2:00 pm is415-385-0049. If any of my skills or experience interests you, please write or phone. Thank you for your time and attention.

Sincerely

Ronald Talbot

(Corrected letters shown on pages 59 and 60)

(BETTER)

1441 Taylor St.
San Francisco, CA 94315
September 28, 19XX

Mr. William Frank
Personnel Director   *mechanics*
ABC Design, Inc.
291 Front St.
San Francisco, Ca., 94128

fragment

← Dear Mr. Frank; :

omit ~~Searching for an employee with qualifications to fit management or a position of responsibility with a degree in adversity.~~ The job description you described in the *Western Placement Annual 1987* is particularly suited to my qualifications. My previous positions in the federal *grammar* government has provided me with skills to ~~overcome~~ *solve* problems and *manifest* myself as an achiever.

vague word sense Mr. Frank, my graduation from Cal State University, Hayward Business Department, in June of '85, has provided me with skills along with my previous employment in government. Hearing your company has an opening in their Marketing and Sales department, I am applying for such a position. Knowing your company deals with a variety of products, I feel that my scope of knowledge of consumer wants and *believe* needs can widen your target market areas. My ability to work with the public and quickly locate their interests makes me a likely candidate.

č strikeover
The enclosed resume will clearly show my qualifications and abilities. ~~Please read for yourself and be the judge.~~

In closing I would appreciate an interview ~~at your convenience~~. Your company office is ~~located~~ near my home, and I would like to meet with you at a time convenient for you. My home phone number after 2:00 pm *Wordy* is 415-385-0049. ~~If any of my skills or experience interests you, please write or phone.~~ Thank you for your time and attention.

Sincerely   *space*

Ronald Talbot

(BEST)

1441 Taylor St.
San Francisco, CA 94315

September 28, 19XX

Mr. William Frank
Personnel Director
ABC Design, Inc.
291 Front St.
San Francisco, CA 94128

Dear Mr. Frank:

I understand that you are searching for an employee with management qualifications. I believe that I am well-suited for the job described in *Western Placement Annual 1987*. I am an achiever with special skills in problem solving.

I graduated from Cal State University, Hayward, with a degree in business in 1985. I have worked as a cost analyst for the federal government for three years. I am applying for the advertised position in your company's Marketing and Sales department. I believe that my knowledge of consumer wants and needs can help you broaden the target markets for your many products. I work well with the public, and I am sure that I can quickly identify their interests.

The enclosed resume will clearly show my qualifications and abilities.

I would appreciate an interview. Your company office is near my home, and I would like to meet with you at a time convenient for you. My home phone number (after 2 p.m.) is (415) 385-0049.

Thank you.

Sincerely,

Ronald Talbot

EXERCISE #23—REVISING A BUSINESS LETTER (2)

Write like a human being, not like a robot. Revise the letter below to give it a more natural, conversational style. Eliminate stock phrases like "enclosed please find," and rewrite stuffy sentences.

(POOR)

Personnel Services Officer
North Coast Community College District
2154 Ridge Drive
Bend, OR 91783

Dear Personnel Services Officer:

Enclosed please find my resume and supporting materials in response to your advertised need for a College Communications Coordinator.

In lieu of a complete written statement which provides my perception of the role of a college communications coordinator I've enclosed reprints of two articles I authored which convey my general feelings about the importance of providing quality educational opportunities which are accessible to as many people as possible.

Briefly, I would add that it is incumbent on spokespersons for public educational institutions to vigorously address the complex public policy and budgetary issues which too often result in decreased tangible fiscal support to public educational institutions.

In addition, it is obviously of primary importance for these same public institutions to make the public aware of the services they provide in order to develop, build and maintain the public participation and support that is essential for the growth of strong and viable public educational institutions.

I would enjoy an opportunity to explore these and other ideas with your organization's leadership and hope to be invited to an interview for that purpose.

Thank you for your consideration.

Sincerely,

Richard Luffkin

(Corrected letters shown on pages 62 and 63)

(BETTER)

August 12, 19XX

Personnel Services Officer
North Coast Community College District
2154 Ridge Drive
Bend, OR 91783

Dear Personnel Services Officer:

cliché Enclosed please find my resume and supporting materials in response to your advertised need for a College Communications Coordinator.

cliché In lieu of a complete written statement which provides my perception of the role of a college communications coordinator I've enclosed reprints of *wrote* two articles I authored which convey my general feelings about the importance of providing quality educational opportunities which are accessible to as many people as possible. *stuffy*

cliché Briefly, I would add that it is incumbent on spokespersons for public educational instituions to vigorously address the complex public policy and budgetary issues which too often result in decreased tangible fiscal support to public educational institutions.

In addition, it is obviously of primary importance for these same public *windy* institutions to make the public aware of the services they provide in order *phrases* to develop, build and maintain the public participation and support that *omit one* is essential for the growth of strong and viable public educational institutions.

I would enjoy an opportunity to explore these and other ideas with your organization's leadership and hope to be invited to an interview for that *passive* purpose.

Thank you for your consideration.

Sincerely,

Richard Luffkin

(BEST)

August 12, 19XX

Personnel Services
North Coast Community College District
2154 Ridge Drive
Bend, OR 91783

I am applying for the position of College Communications Coordinator at
Woodhill College. Enclosed is my resume and several letters of
recommendation.

Instead of a statement on the role of a college communications coordinator, I
am enclosing reprints of two articles I wrote that spell out my strong
feelings about the need for quality education and access for all to these
educational opportunities. I hope you won't mind the substitution.

I believe that people who speak for the colleges have to understand public
policy and the budget. They must be able to explain these issues to
taxpayers in terms they understand, otherwise financial support for the
colleges will continue to erode.

A college information officer's main job is to make the public aware of the
many worthwhile programs and services the college provides. I believe that
providing this information is a vital service, one necessary not only for the
health of the college, but also for continued growth of public education.

I would like to talk with you about these and other matters. I hope you will
invite me for an interview.

Thank you.

Sincerely,

Richard Luffkin

PART VI—THE BUSINESS REPORT

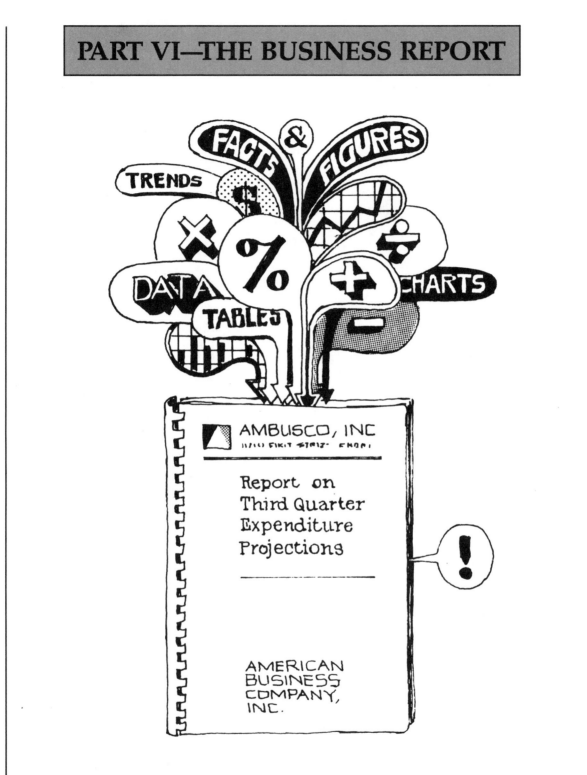

THE BUSINESS REPORT

Organizing a Report

"Have the report on my desk by 3 p.m. Friday." These words can strike terror in the heart of any business writer! Why are business reports and proposals so challenging? For one thing, because usually they are longer and more detailed than memos or letters. Also writers may feel extra pressure because readers may be company officers, co-workers, or important clients. Often the boss will be scrutinizing the writer's words and ideas.

One way to reduce the anxiety of writing a business report is to have a strong organizational plan. A good plan builds confidence. Here are two ways to effectively organize a business report.

Plan #1.   For proposal writing, start with a statement of *what* you are proposing. (State the problem, say why it is important, then say what you are going to do about it.) Next provide whatever background information is necessary. In a third section, analyze the pros and cons of the suggested course of action. Finally, summarize your recommendations.

Plan #2.   For either report or proposal writing, you may also begin with an *overview*. The overview spells out the purpose of the report and the approach it will take. Subsequent sections would cover problem analysis, problem specifics, and budget (if it is a proposal), or past methods, present methods, and evaluation—old vs. new (if it is a report). A final paragraph, a *conclusion*, should be added in either case.

Style Tips

Remember when you write a report that the same language rules apply as in any other form of business writing. Aim for economy, simplicity, and clarity. Keep your sentences short and use familiar words. Direct, clear writing that approximates the way reasonable people speak can never embarrass you.

Revising a Report

Part VI contains a short report for you to revise. Make appropriate changes in language and format, then compare your revision with the improved version on pages 71 and 72.

SOME DO'S AND DON'TS FOR REPORT WRITING

- Determine who will read and evaluate your proposal or report. What are his or her concerns? Tailor your words to specific needs and personalities.

- Follow any existing guidelines (report requirements) to the letter.

- Make an outline.

- Use topic headings, bullets, numbers, and lists. Inset material freely.

- Don't clutter the text with unnecessary tables and graphs. Save those needed for an appendix.

- Longer reports need an abstract (a one page summary) at the beginning.

- Proposals need a cover letter. Keep it brief. Say *why* you are writing, *what* response you want and *when* you want it.

- Be direct and specific, not vague and general. Back up any claims or assertions with facts and figures.

- Don't bury important information in footnotes.

- Be honest about risks and costs. Being straight-forward increases your credibility and undercuts critics.

- Be concise and to the point. Use short paragraphs, concise sentences, and familiar words. Avoid jargon.

- Don't lapse into the cold, stiff, impersonal prose so common in business writing. Switch passive sentences to active and weed out cliches.

EXERCISE #24—REVISING A BUSINESS REPORT

Make appropriate changes to improve this report. The report is well-organized and information is clearly presented. On the other hand you will find some wordy or awkward sentences, a lack of parallelism, and occasionally a poor choice of words.

(POOR)

To: Bill Peterson
          Office Manager

From: Doug Lee
          Head of Accounting

I received your memo, which stated that our company is planning the purchase of some major equipment including a new telephone system, photocopier, computer and word processing system. As you requested, I have spent much time researching to find the types of stystems, which would benefit our company most.

Telephone System

I feel that the best telephone system for our company is the AT&T Touch-a-Matic 1600. The AT&T Touch-a-Matic 1600 was the highest rated telephone in the *Consumer Reports*, January 1987, for small businesses. The Touch-a-Matic costs about $120 per set and includes:
— One- touch dialing for all numbers in memory.
— Has three keys for one-touch dialing emergency calls.
— Has a memory capacity of 15 telephone numbers with 11 digits.
— Handset is of traditional design, for better comfort.
— Digital display for number dialed, ringer off, clocktime, date, and call timer.

Photocopier

My research shows that the best photocopier for our company is the Savin 775. In the *Consumer Reports*, March 1987, the Savin 775 received a high rating for its:
— clear, detailed copying.
— copying in for different colors.
— the many different sizes that can be made on the Savin 775.
The Savin 775 is very compact and would be very easy to move from one office to another. The Savin 775 costs about $750, with a two year warranty, the longest warranty offered on photocopiers.
The length of the warranty combined with the details of the copier, makes me feel that it would be an excellent purchase.

Computer and Word Processing System

I feel that the best computer and word processing system for our company is the IBM Leading Edge Model D. The Leading Edge Model D was picked as the best by the *Consumer Reports*, and *Compute*, both March 1987 issues.

It's a three-piece desktop computer with a price of $1495. Here are some of the features present on the Leading Edge Model D:

— 256K memory, expandable to 640K on motherboard.
— Includes MS-DOS and BASIC software.
— 11-in. TTL monochrome monitor included.
— Leading Edge Word Processor.

The IBM Leading Edge Model D has the clearest graphics and a 15 month warranty, one of the longest offered. I feel that it would be an excellent addition to our company.

Printers

The SP-1000 by Aprotek is the best printer on the market today. The SP-1000 costs about $200, with a two year warranty. The SP-1000 has dot matrix and prints between 20-70 characters per second. It will fit on most computer systems, so it is very convenient.

After lengthy research, I feel that the systems presented in this report will benefit the company the most.

(Improved version on pages 69 through 72)

(BETTER)

To: Bill Peterson
         Office Manager

From: Doug Lee
         Head of Accounting

I received your memo, ~~which~~ stat*ing* that our company is planning the purchase of some major equipment including a new telephone system, photocopier, computer, and word processing system. As you requested, I ~~have spent much time~~ researching to find the types of systems, ~~which~~ *that* would benefit our company most.

Telephone System

believe or think — I ~~feel~~ that the best telephone system for our company is the AT&T Touch-a-Matic 1600. The AT&T Touch-a-Matic 1600 was the highest rated telephone in the *Consumer Reports*, January 1987, *as reported* for small businesses. The Touch-a-Matic costs about $120 per set and includes *three features:*

not parallel
— One- touch dialing for all numbers in memory.
— Has three keys for one-touch dialing emergency calls.
— Has a memory capacity of 15 telephone numbers with 11 digits.
— Handset is of traditional design, for better comfort.
— Digital display for number dialed, ringer off, clocktime, date, and call timer.

Photocopier

My research shows that the best photocopier for our company is the Savin 775. In the *Consumer Reports*, March 1987, the Savin 775 received a high rating for its: *complete sentence should precede colon*

make parallel
— clear, detailed copying.
— copying in ~~for~~ different colors. *sp*
— the many different sizes that can be made on the Savin 775.

wordy — The Savin 775 is ~~very~~ compact and ~~would be very~~ easy to move from ~~one~~ office to ~~another~~ *office*. The Savin 775 costs about $750, with a two-year warranty, the longest warranty offered on photocopiers.

wordy — The length of the warranty combined with the details of the copier makes ~~me feel that~~ it ~~would be~~ an excellent purchase.

70

Computer and Word Processing System

I *feel* that the best computer and word processing system for our company is the IBM Leading Edge Model D. The Leading Edge Model D was *picked* as the best by the *Consumer Reports*, and *Compute*, ~~both~~ March 1987 issues.

think, believe

chosen or selected

It's a three-piece desktop computer ~~with a price of~~ *costing* $1495. Here are some ~~of the~~ features ~~present on~~ the Leading Edge Model D:

parallel?

— 256K memory, expandable to 640K on motherboard.
— Includes MS-DOS and BASIC software.
— 11-in. TTL monochrome monitor included.
— Leading Edge Word Processor.

The IBM Leading Edge Model D has the clearest graphics and a 15 month warranty, one of the longest offered. I *feel* that it would be an excellent addition to our company.

Printers

The SP-1000 by Aprotek is the best printer on the market today. The SP-1000 costs about $200, with a two year warranty. The SP-1000 has dot matrix and prints between 20-70 characters per second. It will fit on most computer systems, so it is very convenient.

After lengthy research, I *feel* that the systems presented in this report will benefit the company the most.

(BEST)

To: Bill Peterson
         Office Manager

From: Doug Lee
         Head of Accounting

I received your memo stating that our company is planning the purchase of some major equipment including a new telephone system, photocopier, computer and word processing system. As you requested, I researched to find the types of systems that would benefit our company most.

Telephone System

I believe that the best telephone systems for our company is the AT&T Touch-a-Matic 1600. The Touch-a-Matic 1600 was the highest rated telephone for small businesses as reported in *Consumer Reports*, January 1987. The Touch-a-Matic costs about $120 per set and includes these features:
— One-touch dialing for all numbers in memory.
— Three keys for one-touch dialing emergency calls.
— A memory capacity of 15 telephone numbers with 11 digits.
— Handset with traditional design for better comfort.
— Digital display for number dialed, ringer off, clocktime, date, and call timer.

Photocopier

My research shows that the best photocopier for our company is the Savin 775. In *Consumer Reports*, March 1987, the Savin 775 received a high rating for several reasons:
— Clear, detailed copying.
— Capacity for copying in four different colors.
— Ability to make copies in many different sizes.
The Savin 775 is compact and easy to move from office to office. The Savin 775 costs about $750, with a two-year warranty, the longest warranty offered on photocopiers.
The length of the warranty combined with the details of the copier make it an excellent purchase.

Computer and Word Processing System

I think that the best computer and word processing system for our company is the IBM Leading Edge Model D. The Leading Edge Model D was selected as the best by both *Consumer Reports*, and *Compute*, March 1987 issues.

It's a three-piece desktop computer costing $1495. Here are some features of the Leading Edge Model D:
— 256K memory, expandable to 640K on motherboard.
— Includes MS-DOS and BASIC software.
— Includes 11 inch TTL monochrome monitor.
— Leading Edge word processor.

The IBM Leading Edge Model D has the clearest graphics and a 15 month warranty, one of the longest offered. I think it would be an excellent addition to our company.

Printers

The SP-1000 by Aprotek is the best printer on the market today. The SP-1000 costs about $200, with a two year warranty. The SP-1000 has dot matrix and prints between 20-70 characters per second. It will fit on most computer systems, so it is very convenient.

After lengthy research, I believe that the systems presented in this report will benefit the company the most.

PART VII—NOW YOU TRY IT!

A Final Challenge

Now it's time to slip some paper into your typewriter, or turn on your word processor, and do some writing of your own. Each exercise in Part VII will direct you to write a memo, letter, or report. Read the instructions and get to work!

EXERCISE #25—WRITING A MEMO (1)

Write a memo to an employee whose work and behavior have been unsatisfactory. (You are the department manager.) Try to motivate the employee to improve his performance. Be brief, direct, honest—and as compassionate and understanding of the feelings of others as possible.

_____

_____

_____

_____

_____

_____

_____

_____

_____

_____

_____

_____

_____

(EXAMPLE)

TO: Gary Cranston

FROM: Pat Hyslop

SUBJECT: Employee Evaluation

DATE: October 16, 19XX

My job is to help you do your job properly. There are a few points I must go over with you.

- Punctuality: Its importance cannot be overstressed. You must be present during normal working hours. If you have a special situation that prevents this, let me know immediately.

- Dress code: Please review *The Employee Handbook* regarding this. As a professional, it's important that you maintain organizational standards concerning appearance.

- Work load: Lately, you have not completed all tasks assigned to you. Perhaps I can assist by helping you set priorities.

Others depend on your contributions. Likewise, we are here for you. If you feel you can use my assistance to improve in the above areas, let me know.

EXERCISE #26—WRITING A MEMO (2)

Write a memo informing clerical employees in an organization about a new procedure, for example, handling incoming mail—where it should be routed, who should handle it, etc.

_____

_____

_____

_____

_____

_____

_____

_____

_____

_____

_____

_____

_____

EXERCISE #27—WRITING A MEMO (3)

Write a memo to inform all office personnel they can no longer smoke at their desks. (You are the office manager.) Tell them where they may smoke, where they may not smoke, and when the policy goes into effect.

_____

_____

_____

_____

_____

_____

_____

_____

_____

_____

_____

_____

_____

EXERCISE #28—WRITING A BUSINESS LETTER (1)

Write a letter of application to a company that has advertised an opening for a job that interests you. Clearly state your interest and qualifications. Be brief and to the point. Be sure to proofread the letter carefully and correct any careless errors.

_____

_____

_____

_____

_____

_____

_____

_____

_____

_____

_____

_____

_____

_____

(EXAMPLE)

May 30, 19XX

231 Summit Av.
Waterloo, IA 93762

William Lynch, Jr.
Communications Systems
Scientific Programing Support
777 Douglas Way
Waterloo, IA 93762

Dear Mr. Lynch:

I am very interested in your department's opening for an entry level
programer. Ted Kilpack, a good friend, told me about the opening. This is
exactly the position I've been looking for.

I have a B.S. in Computer Science from Northridge State College. While at
Northridge, I read of your work with satellites and microwave
communications systems. This is an area of great personal interest, and I
would work hard to be a valuable asset to your department. I am
enclosing my resume which outlines my education and experience.

I would like to interview as soon as possible. I'll call next week to see if
an appointment can be arranged.

Sincerely,

Wayne Larsen

EXERCISE #29—WRITING A BUSINESS LETTER (2)

Write a follow-up letter thanking a customer for his or her business. The letter should be brief, direct, and courteous.

_____

_____

_____

_____

_____

_____

_____

_____

_____

_____

_____

_____

_____

(EXAMPLE)

CLEAN-DRY
of San Ramon County
Carpet, Upholstery & Drapery Cleaning
156 North Industrial Road
San Carlos, CA 94031

May 6, 19XX

Dear Customer:

We at CLEAN-DRY appreciate your recent business, and we hope you were happy with our work.

Over the years, we have worked hard to establish a reputation for quality service. This has been done with the help of customer referrals. If you were pleased with our work and price, we would appreciate your passing the enclosed discount certificates on to your friends and neighbors. Remember to keep one for yourself for future use.

Again, thank you for the pleasure of serving you.

Sincerely,

Jack Keller
Owner

EXERCISE #30—WRITING A BUSINESS LETTER (3)

Write a letter to a potential customer for a firm's products or services. Attempt to convince the client to make a purchase. Be as persuasive as possible. Give the client several good reasons for making the purchase. Tell the client how the transaction will benefit sales, reduce costs, or eliminate problems.

_____

_____

_____

_____

_____

_____

_____

_____

_____

_____

_____

_____

_____

(EXAMPLE)

Stanley Rose
Fitrite Pants
589 Hennepin Av.
Minneapolis, MN 56429

Dear Stan:

I am prepared to write an insertion order for an ad in the *Post* for Fitrite Pants anytime you give the word. I am confident that by putting your message before our 600,000 readers you will see an immediate impact on sales.

As you know, the *Post* is the only morning newspaper in the metropolitan area with that kind of circulation.

By signing a contract now, you will qualify for our special May incentive plan. Instead of our usual retail display rate of $18.50 a column inch, you will pay just $14.50, a savings of over twenty percent.

Also, Bill Smith, our best copy and layout man, has suggested a way of making further savings without reducing impact. Bill's idea is to run one column rather than two column ads but increase the boldness of the headline type. Bill will be pleased to assist you should you decide to sign our contract.

When we talked last week I provided a list of current clients as references. I've worked especially closely with Murray Levitz and Ted Larson this past year. You might want to give them a call. Murray knows Bill Smith's work, too, as Bill does the ads for SuperSaver.

I'll call you Monday to make an appointment and show you the new one column layouts.

Sincerely,

Tom Cowles

EXERCISE #31—WRITING A BUSINESS REPORT

Write a report proposing a solution to a problem that has been identified by management of a company or agency. Your report should be three to four pages in length. Organize your report clearly and logically. Give each section an appropriate heading. You may use the following outline to plan your report, or make your own outline.

    A. Problem

    B. Recommendation

    C. Rationale

    D. Alternative Solutions

    E. Appendix (Data)

(EXAMPLE)

TO: Mr. Charles P. Wentworth

FROM: Scott Hemingway, Resident Manager

DATE: March 2, 1987

SUBJECT: Recommended promotion to decrease high vacancy rate

Problem

Oak Park Villa currently has three vacancies. Two out of the last three tenants moved out because of high rents. When prospective tenants come to see the units, they seem very excited. However, with numerous vacancy signs in the general area, they soon find a similar unit for less money.

Recommendation

Attached is a market analysis of nine similar townhome rentals in Centerville. According to the analysis, the average monthly rent for a two bedroom townhome is $780.56. We have been asking $850.

My recommendation would be to adjust rents down to market level by offering a month's free rent for all those signing a year lease. However, instead of giving the first month's rent free, we should prorate it throughout the last six months of the first year. The promotion would be $850 for the first six months and $720 for the last six. We would also offer this promotion to current tenants wishing to sign for another year.

Rationale

Offering a month's free rent is beneficial for several reasons:
- It should reduce the length of time needed to rent a vacant unit, increasing rent revenue.
- It should reduce the number of vacancies by encouraging current tenants to renew their contracts.
- It is flexible. When demand for townhome rentals increases, the promotion can simply be reduced or eliminated for all future tenants.
- It keeps the cash inflow stable by distributing the discount throughout a six month period.

Rejected Alternatives

Other alternatives to the vacancy problem are to do nothing, to increase advertising, to lower rents, or to offer a free gift as another form of promotion.

Doing nothing is not a solution. With three vacancies, doing nothing costs $85 a day in lost rent revenues. This equals $2,550 a month or $30,600 a year. The promotion should reduce average vacancies to less than one a month. Even with "free rent," a reduction to one vacancy would increase rent revenue by at least $10,400 and perhaps $20,800.

Increasing advertising is not a solution unless we have something *special* to offer. If we promote a month's free rent, more advertising would be beneficial. Otherwise, advertising just emphasizes our higher rents compared to similar units.

Lowering the monthly rent is a possible alternative. However, people like to receive discounts. A month's free rent is much more enticing and is an appropriate award for those signing a year lease.

Offering a free gift is not always effective. Offering a free VCR or free lottery tickets may help reduce the vacancy rate, but this does not always work. If the gift is not needed nor desired by the prospective tenant, it offers no motivation. The most appropriate gift for any tenant is free rent. Giving a month's free rent prorated throughout the last six months offers savings but at less risk. There always exists the possibility that a tenant cannot or will not complete his year lease. Prorating the rent will discourage this from happening. However, if the tenant does abandon, losses are minimized.

Market Analysis of Comparable Units

DEVELOPMENT	RENT	SQ FT	BEDRMS	BTHRMS	POOL	FIREPL	GARAGE	VACANCY	PROMOTION
Oak Park Villa	**$850**	**1100**	**2**	**1.5**	**Yes**	**Yes**	**No**	**3**	**?**
The Village	750	950	2	1.5	Yes	Yes	No	1	None
Westwood	760	950	2	1.5	Yes	No	Yes	0	1 Mo Free
Elm Tree Villa	825	1100	2	1.5	Yes	No	Yes	1	None
Gatewood	650	930	2	1.5	No	No	No	0	None
Fairoaks	795	990	2	1.5	Yes	Yes	No	2	None
Del Greco	895	1300	3	2.0	No	No	Yes	2	None
Park Village	825	1100	2	1.5	Yes	Yes	No	1	1 Mo Free
Continental	750	1100	2	1.5	Yes	No	No	0	None
Los Padres	775	1230	2	1.5	Yes	Yes	Yes	1	None

Average Rent: $780.56

NOTES

NOW AVAILABLE FROM CRISP PUBLICATIONS

Books • Videos • CD Roms • Computer-Based Training Products

Subject Areas Include:

Management

Human Resources

Communication Skills

Personal Development

Marketing/Sales

Organizational Development

Customer Service/Quality

Computer Skills

Small Business and Entrepreneurship

Adult Literacy and Learning

Life Planning and Retirement

CRISP WORLDWIDE DISTRIBUTION

English language books are distributed worldwide. Major international distributors include:

ASIA/PACIFIC

Australia/New Zealand: In Learning, PO Box 1051 Springwood QLD, Brisbane, Australia 4127
Telephone: 7-3841-1061, Facsimile: 7-3841-1580   ATTN: Messrs. Gordon

Singapore: Graham Brash (Pvt) Ltd. 32, Gul Drive, Singapore 2262
Telephone: 65-861-1336, Facsimile: 65-861-4815   ATTN: Mr. Campbell

CANADA

Reid Publishing, Ltd., Box 69559-109 Thomas Street, Oakville, Ontario Canada L6J 7R4.
Telephone: (905) 842-4428, Facsimile: (905) 842-9327   ATTN: Mr. Reid

Trade Book Stores: Raincoast Books, 8680 Cambie Street, Vancouver, British Columbia, Canada V6P 6M9.
Telephone: (604) 323–7100, Facsimile: 604-323-2600   ATTN: Ms. Laidley

EUROPEAN UNION

England: Flex Training, Ltd. 9-15 Hitchin Street, Baldock, Hertfordshire, SG7 6A, England
Telephone: 1-462-896000, Facsimile: 1-462-892417   ATTN: Mr. Willetts

INDIA

Multi-Media HRD, Pvt., Ltd., National House, Tulloch Road, Appolo Bunder, Bombay, India 400-039
Telephone: 91-22-204-2281, Facsimile: 91-22-283-6478   ATTN: Messrs. Aggarwal

MIDDLE EAST

United Arab Emirates: Al-Mutanabbi Bookshop, PO Box 71946, Abu Dhabi
Telephone: 971-2-321-519, Facsimile: 971-2-317-706   ATTN: Mr. Salabbai

SOUTH AMERICA

Mexico: Grupo Editorial Iberoamerica, Serapio Rendon #125, Col. San Rafael, 06470 Mexico, D.F.
Telephone: 525-705-0585, Facsimile: 525-535-2009   ATTN: Señor Grepe

SOUTH AFRICA

Alternative Books, Unit A3 Sanlam Micro Industrial Park, Hammer Avenue STRYDOM Park, Randburg, 2194 South Africa
Telephone: 2711 792 7730, Facsimile: 2711 792 7787   ATTN: Mr. de Haas